Emergency Vehicles

By Penelope Arlon
and Tory Gordon-Harris

Discover even more with your free digital companion book.

vrooom!

emergency vehicles fun!

enter

SCHOLASTIC discover more

Fun activities!

Sounds!

1 **one** rescue boat — rescue boat
2 **two** sirens — siren
3 **three** lights — light
4 **four** tires — tire
5 **five** helmets — helmet
home

six firefighters — firefighter
7 **seven** motorcycles — motorcycle
8 **eight** helicopters — helicopter
9 **nine** patrol cars — patrol car
10 **ten** fire trucks — fire truck
twe... ambulance

20

Infopops!

Videos!

The busy ambulance

Ambulances have powerful engines so they can speed paramedics to the scene.

Paramedics learn to drive under pressure.

home

light

side door

PARAMEDICS

sign in reverse

AMBULANCE

PARAMEDICS

look

See a busy ambulance at work.

listen

What sound does an ambulance make?

To download your free digital book, visit **www.scholastic.com/discovermore**

Enter this code: RMJGCPF4WDX9

Contents

Literacy Consultant: Barbara Russ, 21st Century Community Learning Center Director for Winooski (Vermont) School District

Copyright © 2013 by Scholastic Inc.

All rights reserved. Published by Scholastic Inc., *Publishers since 1920.*
SCHOLASTIC, SCHOLASTIC DISCOVER MORE™, and associated logos are trademarks and/or registered trademarks of Scholastic Inc.

Library of Congress Cataloging-in-Publication Data Available

ISBN 978-0-545-49563-9

10 9 8 7 6 5 4 3 2   13 14 15 16 17

Printed in Malaysia   108
First edition, January 2013

Scholastic is constantly working to lessen the environmental impact of our manufacturing processes.
To view our industry-leading paper procurement policy, visit www.scholastic.com/paperpolicy.

Emergency!

If you need help, emergency vehicles are always ready to rush to the rescue.

To call for help, dial 911.

Land rescue

Police cars transport police officers to accidents.

Motorcycles can whiz through traffic to reach an emergency.

Special fire trucks are used at airports for airplane fires.

Sea rescue

Air rescue

Airplanes and helicopters can search from the air or reach remote areas.

Fire trucks are fully equipped to put out fires and to rescue.

The police sometimes have to use vehicles that can go off road.

Ambulances are like mini-hospitals on wheels.

Many different boats are used for sea rescues. They often work closely with air vehicles.

RNLI 16-09

Superspeedy police cars are often the first vehicles at an emergency.

A police officer can check out a car or person right away, using the computer in the police car.

Police cars have very powerful engines to make them extra fast.

POLICE LINE DO NO

Australia

Poland

China

Italy

Police cars all have markings that make them easy to spot. Different countries use their own colors and markings.

first-aid kit, tools, and body armor in trunk

CROSS

Police vehicles

Police don't just drive cars; they use lots of other vehicles, too.

Police cruise the roads on their motor trikes.

Mobile control units have offices inside of them.

The quickest way around a busy city may be by bike.

River police use Jet Skis to patrol waterways.

If there is a traffic jam, police motorcycles can rush through quickly, straight to an accident.

Sometimes police patrol the streets on Segways.

Riverboats are a speedy way to cross a busy city.

Horses are often used to control crowds of people.

Police buses transport criminals to prison.

Sky police

Emergency! A criminal is on the loose. A police helicopter takes to the air.

The police helicopter guides police cars on the ground toward the criminal.

A camera beneath the helicopter films the ground so that the crew and police headquarters can watch the action.

camera

A heat-sensitive camera can locate a person or car at night without using a light.

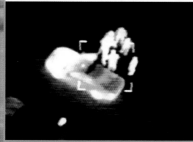

When a criminal is spotted, a powerful searchlight follows his or her every move.

The police sometimes use loudspeakers to talk to the criminal they are tracking.

Fire!

A fire truck carries lots of equipment, such as cutting tools, floodlights, breathing apparatus, and extra hoses.

There's a fire—call out the fire truck!

hose

ax

The fire truck has its own water tank. It can also suck up more water from a hydrant or even a swimming pool.

A ladder is raised to allow firefighters to spray close to a fire and rescue people.

Firefighters on the ground spray the fire with water.

Firefighters can also spray water from the top of the ladder.

Fireboat

When there is a fire at sea, fireboats rush to the rescue over the waves.

burning tanker

OC-13

Help! There's a fire on an oil rig out at sea. Call the fireboat!

The fireboat arrives, filled with emergency and medical supplies.

It carries foam, which it sprays to put out the burning oil.

Some fireboats take water from the sea, so they can spray water for hours.

Fireboats can pump water 400 feet (122 m) into the air.

fireboat

15

Superscooper

There's a forest fire!
Watch for this amazing
airplane that scoops
and drops water.

A Superscooper can drop water up to 9 times an hour.

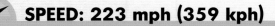

The Superscooper flies down to open water and scoops it up for 12 seconds.

Without stopping, the airplane zooms back up into the sky, toward the fire.

The plane is tough enough to handle big gusts of wind that blow above a fire.

17

Lifeboat

Accidents at sea normally happen in bad weather, so lifeboats have to be tough.

A lifeboat carries a lot of equipment to take care of cold, wet, or injured people.

life preserver

blanket

first-aid kit

If this lifeboat tips over in the huge waves, it turns itself upright immediately.

A tractor moves the lifeboat on land.

Sea rescue

Mayday! A distress call at sea is received. Launch the lifeboats!

Help!

A boat has capsized, or turned over. The crew makes a distress call and inflates a small life raft in the sea.

Launch

The lifeboat station receives the Mayday signal, or distress call, and the lifeboat is launched down a ramp.

This small inflatable lifeboat can launch from and land on a beach.

Sailors may set off a distress flare to show the lifeboat where they are.

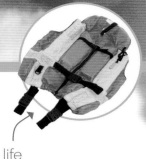

life jacket

On the way

Small inflatable boats can be launched from the main lifeboat. They are speedy and can pick up passengers easily.

Rescue

Underwater rescuers may wear NewtSuits. A diver in a NewtSuit can dive to depths of 820 feet (250 m).

Rescue workers wear life jackets and helmets.

Air-sea rescue

Passenger overboard!
Send in the air and
sea rescue teams.

ROYAL NAV
RESCU

A rescue helicopter
works closely with
lifeboats in a sea
emergency.

Some types of
helicopter can take
off from and land
on water.

An injured person can
be winched up on a
stretcher to travel back
to land by helicopter.

COAST GUARD

A rescue
swimmer may
be lowered into
the sea to help.

Ambulance

medic
motorcycle

When someone is suddenly ill or injured, an ambulance is called. I hear a siren—let the ambulance through!

An ambulance sounds its siren and flashes its lights so that other motorists get out of the way.

An emergency center receives a 911 call and takes details.

An ambulance, full of medical equipment, races off to the rescue.

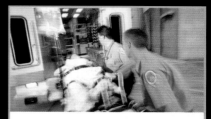

A very sick person is rushed to a local hospital for treatment.

Paramedics, trained to deal with medical emergencies, drive and ride in the ambulance.

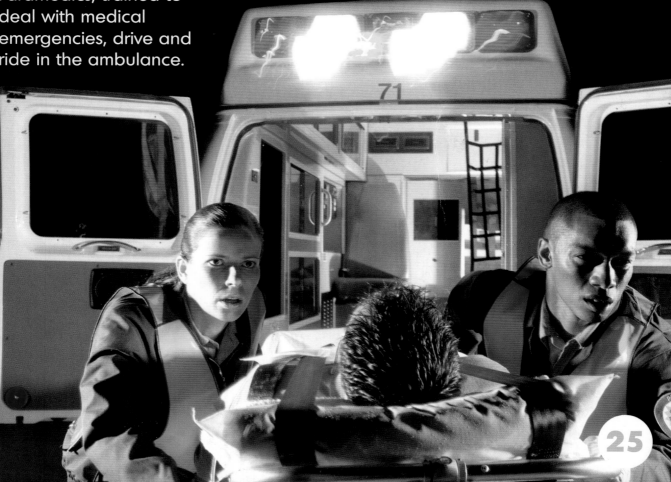

Flying doctors

If a road vehicle can't get to a sick patient, flying doctors take to the skies.

height:
35,000 feet (10,670 m)

An air ambulance carries a pilot, a doctor, and a nurse.

In Australia, many people live far away from a hospital.

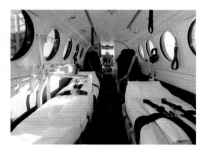

An air ambulance, filled with medical equipment, flies to pick up a patient.

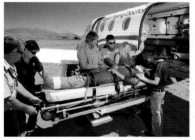

The patient has to be strapped on to a stretcher to keep from bumping around.

Monitors on the plane send ahead information about the patient to a hospital.

A road ambulance waits on the runway to take the patient to the nearest hospital.

Search and rescue

Whether up a mountain, on ice, or in a swamp, there is always an emergency vehicle ready for action.

A hydrocopter can travel over ice, across water, through snow, and even over land.

Mountain

A helicopter is sometimes the only vehicle that can rescue people from a steep mountain.

Sea

Seaplanes can take off from and land on water. They can rescue lots of people at once.

Flood

Airboats have very flat bottoms, so they are perfect for rescues in swampy areas or floods.

Ice and snow

In icy Arctic seas, where neither boats nor cars can travel, a hydrocopter rushes to the rescue.

Glossary

Arctic
The very cold area around the North Pole.

breathing apparatus
Equipment worn by rescuers that allows them to breathe fresh air through smoke.

capsize
To become overturned, especially a boat.

distress flare
A blaze of light or smoke that is set off to attract attention.

floodlight
A light that produces a wide beam.

heat-sensitive camera
A camera that detects body heat and turns it into images that can be seen on a computer.

hydrant
A pipe to a main water supply, with a nozzle for attaching a hose when fighting fires.

life preserver
A ring or belt that floats in water and can be used to keep a person from sinking.

It often takes two firefighters to hold and steady the hose.

Mayday
The word used as a distress call over a radio. This word is used all over the world.

paramedic
A person trained to give emergency medical help before or during a trip to a hospital.

patient
Someone who is ill and being treated by a doctor.

siren
A machine that makes a loud sound to warn people about something.

stretcher
A flat, portable bed that is used to carry a sick or injured person.

winch
To lift or pull an object using a machine that has rope, cable, or chain wound around a roller.

A firefighter wraps a child in an emergency blanket to keep the child warm.

Index

Thank you

Art Director: Bryn Walls
Designer: Ali Scrivens
Managing Editor: Miranda Smith
Managing Production Editor: Stephanie Engel
US Editor: Esther Lin
Cover Designer: Neal Cobourne
DTP: John Goldsmid
Digital Photography Editor: Stephen Chin
Visual Content Project Manager: Diane Allford-Trotman
Executive Director of Photography, Scholastic: Steve Diamond

Photography
1: George Doyle/Thinkstock; 3: mladn61/iStockphoto; 4–5 (background): Smit/Shutterstock; 4tr: George Doyle & Ciaran Griffin/Thinkstock; 4cl: Tupungato/Dreamstime; 4cm: Oleksiy Maksymenko Photography/Alamy; 4cr: Ron Brown/SuperStock; 4bc: Faraways/Shutterstock; 4br: Thinkstock; 5tl: Tupungato/Shutterstock; 5tc: VMJones/iStockphoto; 5tr: Jupiterimages/Thinkstock; 5cl: ryasick/iStockphoto; 5cm: Albert Campbell/Shutterstock; 5cr: Comstock/Thinkstock; 5bl: Jinny Goodman/Alamy; 5br: RNLI/Nicholas Leach; 6–7 (background): Kellie L. Folkerts/Shutterstock; 6–7 (police tape): carl ballou/Shutterstock; 6tc: Media Bakery; 7tl: Tupungato/Dreamstime; 7tcl: Rkaphotography/Dreamstime; 7tcr: Zhongfei Li/Dreamstime; 7tr: Korisei/Dreamstime; 7br: Zhou Peng/Dreamstime; 8t: Simon

Hadley/Alamy; 8bl: Bill Scott/Getty Images; 8bcl: JFLAURIN/iStockphoto; 8bcr: Loic Bernard/iStockphoto; 8br: Jack Sullivan/Alamy; 9t: Oleksiy Maksymenko Photography/Alamy; 9bl: Media Bakery; 9bcl: AdShooter/iStockphoto; 9bcr: Eugene Hoshiko/Associated Press; 9br: CulturalEyes-AusSoc/Alamy; 10–11: Mario Tama/Getty Images; 11tr: Spacephotos/age fotostock; 11bl: SHOUT/Alamy; 11bc: David McNew/Getty Images; 11br, 12tl: Thinkstock; 12bl: Hemera/Thinkstock; 12–13 (fire truck): ryasick/iStockphoto; 13 (fire and ladder): Kazela/Shutterstock; 13tc: iStockphoto/Thinkstock; 13tr: Hemera/Thinkstock; 13bc: Shaun Lowe/iStockphoto; 13br: iStockphoto/Thinkstock; 14–15: RIA Novosti/Photo Researchers, Inc.; 15tl: Leo Francini/Shutterstock; 15tc: iStockphoto/Thinkstock; 15tr: Photo Researchers, Inc.; 16–17 (background and plane r): Kevork Djansezian/Associated Press; 16 (plane): nadirco/Shutterstock; 17tl, 17tr: ChinellatoPhoto/Shutterstock; 18–19: Bob Barnes/Alamy; 19tl: iStockphoto/Thinkstock; 19tc: Mark Stout/Thinkstock; 19tr: pagadesign/iStockphoto; 20cl: Tobias Bernhard/Corbis; 20cr: marc macdonald/Alamy; 20–21 (lifeboat and water): Bob Barnes/Alamy; 21tl: Dick Luria/Thinkstock; 21tr: Stockbyte/Thinkstock; 21cl: Roy Childs/Alamy; 21cr: Alexis Rosenfeld/Photo Researchers, Inc.; 21br: keith morris/Alamy; 22–23: RNLI/Sam Jones; 22cl: iStockphoto/Thinkstock; 22cm: United States Coast Guard; 22cr: iStockphoto/Thinkstock; 24tl: one-image photography/Alamy; 24b: George Doyle/Thinkstock; 25tl: Comstock/Thinkstock; 25tc: Hemera/Thinkstock; 25tr: Comstock/Thinkstock; 25b: Stockbyte/Thinkstock; 26–27: State Library of Western Australia; 27cl, 27cm, 27cr: Royal Flying Doctors Service; 27b: Robert Harding Picture Library/SuperStock; 28–29: Arctic Ant Ltd; 28bl, 28br: iStockphoto/Thinkstock; 29bl: Bill Haber/Associated Press; 29br: Arctic Ant Ltd; 30: Peter Hvizdak/The Image Works; 31: Michael Courtney/iStockphoto.

Cover
Front cover: (tl) Daniel Cardiff/iStockphoto; (tr) Cafebeanz Company/Dreamstime; (c) Terifrancis/Dreamstime; (c background) javarman/Shutterstock.
Back cover: (computer monitor) Manaemedia/Dreamstime.